WITCH

LISSA GRACEY

WITH A STORY BY
LEENA KARJALAINEN

Acknowledgements

Versions of "Autumn Equinox", "Valentine Moon", "The Hill of the Witch", "Winter Solstice, Long Meg", "Starlings" and "Samhain" have been previously published in the poetry magazine "Moonstone" (produced for 26 years from Settle in Yorkshire, which sadly stopped publication at Samhain 2005), under the name of Alison Matthews.

Copyright © Lissa Gracey 2023

All rights reserved.

Except for brief quotations in critical articles or reviews, no part of this book may be used or reproduced without the written consent of the copyright owner.

For Keith, Emma, Tom and Leena

and witches everywhere

Who were the witches? Where did they come from?
Maybe your great, great grandmother was one?
Witches were wise wise women they say
and there's a little witch in every woman today.

Bonnie Lockhart

CONTENTS

Witch	3
The Elements	5
Earth	6
Air	7
Fire	8
Water	9
Ether	10
The Wheel of the Year	11
Samhain	12
Two Moons	13
Two Moons	15
The Last Wolf	16
Starlings	18
A Murmuration	19
Solstice	20
Winter Solstice, Long Meg	21
Long Meg	22
Dreams	23
Stone	24
Imbolc	26
Valentine Moon	27
Aztec	29
Where Are You Going?	30
Blue Fish	31
Tattoo Parlour	33
Spring Orchids	34
Spring Equinox, Haweswater	35
Mother	36

Beltane	37
The Year of the Tiger	38
Midsummer	40
Lady of the Links	41
I Could Fly	43
Ta Prohm	44
Ta Prohm	*45*
Climbing, Floating, Flying	46
Stone Forest I & Stone Forest II	48
The Hill of the Witch	49
Do You Remember?	50
The House at Päiväranta	*52*
Memories of a Finnish Childhood	53
The Sauna at Päiväranta	*56*
Mad Cow Island (Leena Karjalainen)	57
Memories of Childhood	*59*
Sycorax	60
Autumn Equinox	62
Roar Like a Lion	63
Companions	64
The Journey	65
Immram	67
Hecate	69
We Are The Witches	70

Witch

Witch
bitch
not a stitch
hedge flyer
owl crier
foul hag   charm bag
ragwort sticks   River Styx
stick in pins
rag doll moll
Black Jack   Man-in-Black
toad   imp   pimp   whore
henbane   wolf's bane   poison lore
brew of newt and hemlock root
stew-pot   storm-pot
hare hop   toad plop
three drops
blight a crop
in a blink   take a drink
viper's sting   kill a king
deadly nightshade   ring a bell
ride an egg-shell
go to hell.

Witch
rich
earth wisdom witch
wort cunning
rune running
rune chanter   enchanter
star stalker   spirit talker
journey-between-the-worlds walker
allheal   starry wheel

yarrow stalk   fire walk
lone crone   holey stone
holy smoke   sacred oak
whirling dervish   whirl of power
crystal castle   turning tower
young old wild bold
keeper of secrets never told
west of the moon   east of the sun
dance the mill   the spell's begun
ice fire sky water
she is the mist and moon's daughter
wolf howl   cat on the prowl
shaper
shifter
bone sifter
past the spiral
through the tomb
into the darkness
of the womb.

The Elements

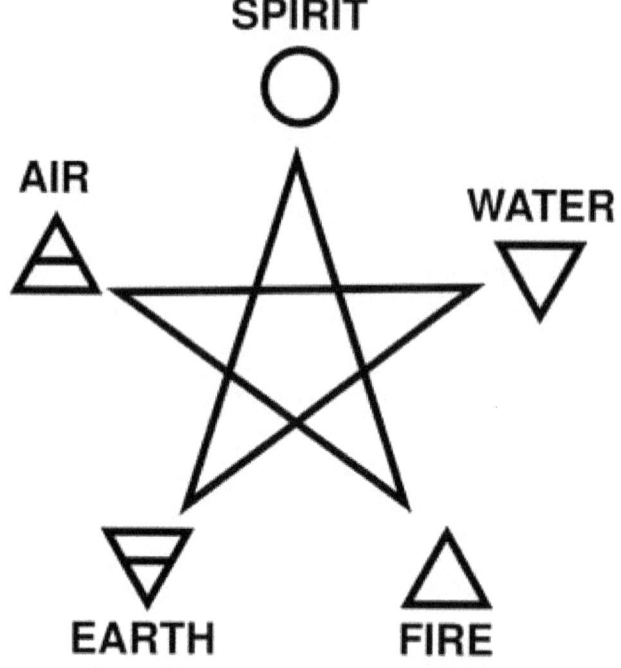

Earth

My beauty shimmers
as I spin
in endless space –
I am a sapphire
in a boundless brow
precious beyond measure;
I am the Kingdom
that you seek –
in my dear flesh
plunge deep the roots
of that eternal Tree.
My virgin breasts
nourish you; I run
with milk and honey.
I hold you
in my arms, woo you
with my beauty;
I am your bride: yet
I am the Gate of Tears,
the Gate of Death.
A drum beats deep
within the caverns
of my heart,
making the atoms
of your soul
dance and spin
in their small universe.
I tremble with that pulse,
hold tight the pain
and passion of my being.
I can guide you
down the radiant path
if you will give
yourself to me.

Air

I am a swan's sigh
sweet as a fivefold kiss
of womb and lip. The sky
holds my breath in her soft lap
and pours my soul
into her starry cup.

I am the passion
of Shu; I spawn children
Sky and Earth, and fashion
wings of dew and dust and space
to hold apart
their wild embrace.

I am harbinger
of death in dying worlds;
my sour poison lingers
in my gaseous mouth, fingers
skeletons of stone
and oceans dried to bone.

Cherubic, I blow
my breath four ways, to wax,
wane, warm, chill; rock to and fro
life's crib, flap and crack the sails
of this frail barque
straining, streaming to the dark.

Fire

I flicker at the edge of dreams;
I smoke behind your eyes
and smoulder in the skull.
I am the keeper of visions –
I make you fly.
Sing songs of dragons
and I will dance in your soul,
stoke your heart
and stir your belly with
the tongues of snakes.
But if you slay them
I will rage beneath the skin,
boil in the bowels of earth,
spew seas of glass and ash;
I will consume you.

I am born of stars
flaming in galactic space –
I forge my crucible
from countless suns
and temper blades that flash
across the universe.
I change everything I touch.
I am invincible.
Endless.
Terrible.

Water

I am water, gentle
as moths' wings, cocooning
your skin with silk; softly
I soothe, protect, tremble
at your finger ends, scatter
my radiance like thistledown.

I am water, sombre
as the grave, delving deep
into your soul's abyss.
Fathom by dread fathom
I penetrate the dark pit
of your secret innermost core.

I am water, thunderous
I wield my hefty hammers
like some fierce north god, pounding
earth's flesh; with Baba's pestle
I grind the skeleton bones
of men and mighty mountains.

I am water, sacred
to the Mother of all things –
Don, Boann, great Ganga,
destroyer and creatrix;
in my mortar the matrix
and mystery of life and death.

Ether

Ether is the fifth element.
Spirit. Energy. Heart.
A mystery.
Some say it's love.
Can you hold it in your cupped hands
before it slips away?

I've tried to catch its essence
but it twists and turns
like the river, surging over stones,
shrouding the island
where cormorants bask
in sunny weather.

Maybe in spring, when catkins
swing their tails and buds
burst from the cage of winter
I will seize it. It will fill me
as the rising sun blazes
across mountains.

A heartsong.

The Wheel of the Year

Samhain

Samhain:
the year's end.
Trees are still ablaze –
sulphurous maples pulse
their acrid glow, oaks
burn and shimmer. Birch
cascades her speckled gold
and rowan bleeds her jewels,
crimson in the ebbing sun. Scorched
leaves crunch beneath our reckless feet,
while overhead a slow heron wings west,
homeward, a dark phoenix risen from
our souls' embers. The bonfire smoke
curls, wisps, puffs, shoots ash into the
burnished air, carrying our hopes, fears,
failures and successes, things done
and undone, pains and joys, up
up into Arianrhod's bright spiral.
And in that space which is no space
between year's end and year's
beginning, we glimpse our past
and future –we spin with
vast stars, circle
fiery nebulae;
we become
incandescent
immortal
infinite

Two Moons

Tonight
there are two moons.

One floats in water
like a pool of cream
spilt in a silver dish;
the other cradled
in the velvet glove of sky,
so bright, the stars are dim-
and all is still
save the soft lap
of water at the lake's brim.

I will frolic
in the water moon,
join nymphs and nixies
in their play,
ride water dragons
and sing sweet, sad songs
with sprites and sirens
in the reeds.

Until
I hear a cry,
a harsh call
from the wild wood-
and tides turn
in my veins and bones.

Then I will prowl
beneath the sky moon
and howl with wolves

in forests of the night-
I will run free
beside others of my kind,
visit goblins
ride unicorns
weave spells with witches, elves
until the moons set
and I can seek my rest ...

Tonight
There are two moons.

Two Moons

The Last Wolf

I howl to the moon
but her ice-cold stare
shows no pity. No pity.
Over moor and fell I fled the cries
of my pursuers, on paths that sang
with my ancestors' blood, throbbed
to the beat of a ghost tribe's heart.
I slipped through dark trees: oak, ash, yew
gathered like shades waiting to enter
Hel's realm, haunting the places
of joy and terror. I sorrowed
and raged to feel the musk-soft earth
and fragrant grass, the tender hollow
where we mated under a moon
kinder and luminous in her blessing;
the crook of land where our young
nestled, fur-snug, played and fought
mock battles in blade-sharp mornings.
The place of execution.
There was no birdsong. No song.
A steel-eyed hunter wore my mate's pelt
around his shoulders.

I have run my course to the brink
of the world. Below the crag's tip
sea smokes over mud
brown as winter bracken.
Thorn trees slant, shorn by storm
and the dawn sky arches, pales, ends here.
I am alone. I am ready.

My cry will echo with the wild
call of gulls, the keening wind.
My breath will dance in the atoms
of these grey stones.

*The last wolf in England was reputedly killed at Humphrey Head,
overlooking Morecambe Bay, in about 1390.*

Starlings

Dusk. Gold threads stitch the sky.
Cloud scraps scud and scatter
as the boom and thud of the world-loom's beater
punches the drum-tight fabric, smooth as a skull.

High on the hill's breast, the Three
spin, twirling the light spindle, measure
moist breath of watchful dragons, and cut
the sheer, taut cloth swaddling Earth's bare bones.

Through the frayed edge of the warp's portal
strange stars span a universe unknown;
a soft heart-murmur thrums and swells
the cosmic waves lapping a faraway shore,

until suddenly they breach the gap,
crashing the barrier, to whirr and wheel
the wild air, skeining the wind,
dancing the Witches' Rune until they drop.

So, with ten thousand murmuring wings,
I have heard and seen eternity
beating its web, spinning its song,
humming, flying, flowing between the worlds.

A Murmuration

Solstice

Holly bears a berry like a bead of blood,
a crown of thorns as sharp as splintered bone.
Now when the earth is silent as a tomb
we see the void, the dark, the death of light
and mourn the year's passing; we wait
in trepidation for a sign, a sacrifice, a birth.

Some say a child came with a star
who later bled with thorns and rose from the dead;
others, our sun was reborn from the blood of bulls
to ride glorious in a chariot of flame.

I only trust that light will rise again, and penetrate
the inner chamber, strike the pillar, flood the world with hope,
while thorns protect new shoots
and berries bear the seeds of spring.

Winter Solstice, Long Meg

Earth quivers, and at her rim
the membranes break
splashing pools of topaz
a show of eastern rubies
streaking the sky's bowl.
The midwife ash
stoops bare and grey
succouring crabbed hands bent
like witches' fingers, black-nailed, life-giving.

Slowly he comes, the pale new sun,
as earth sighs, crowning between
the dark hills of her thighs.
On her outbreath a crow calls
and Venus throbs, portents
of the nativity.
The wise attentive stones
whisper incantations, weave their spells,
spin a brittle thread
of life and destiny, guardians
of the mystery
from times before and after Ragnarok.

Weakly he rests, suspended
on earth's navel
until, cord cut, he lifts and soars
milky and radiant
flooding the fields
with rosy frankincense and gold,
warming the wyrd web
nursing the world tree
turning the stones' spindle –
an unconquered newborn god.

Long Meg

Dreams

There is a secret stair
down to the cavern of dreams.
Here is everything we wish or fear –
a path of bones, an angel's wing,
a whisper of moon, a sky with clouds as fair
as pearls seeded on a string.

But deeper still are streams
of shadows, dark mirrors pitched
into the living sea of waking dreams,
where terrors and wonders of the deep
reflect our inner selves, where seems
our souls are weighed and sunk in sleep.

In this strange place
all is illusion;
we meet our nemesis, whose face
is so familiar, yet unknown.
Strangers greet us at the edge of space
before we return home alone.

With acknowledgement to John Clare

Stone

This stone
is so black
it oozes
from the furnace
of my heart.
I am afraid
of its denseness
its solidity
the smooth darkness
of its being
shiny as a beetle
each atom winged
and creeping slowly
in my ribs.
I am old
Cailleach
hag woman
and the stone
sits heavy in me
crushing my breath
now filling me
rippling out
from my centre;
an ocean
of atoms.
I am turning
to stone –
each fibre
each molecule
of my being
vibrates with

the slow beat
of its blackness.
Yet inside
I am vast space
I have caverns
of darkness
in me
I feel enormous
as a cathedral.
Maybe
I will expand
to fill
the universe.

Imbolc

Ice blades crack.
Streams, like sacred knives,
cut the swollen soil
to plunge into the river chalice.
Air and water blessedly conjoined -
ritual of consummation.
Fat sheep graze, placid, smug,
bellies tight as cauldrons
as deep within Annwyn
flutters the first pulse of blood,
a surge of seed and shoot
quickening the ancient mill,
arousing the dark hag
from her cold slumber.
Sacrament of flesh and earth.
Above, willow buds swell gold;
stones turn on their spindle
and grass spears sparkle.
The hooded chrysalis
splits from end to end.
Hail Etain, bright damsel!
Hail Brid, forged of flame!
Metamorphosis of fire.

Valentine Moon

Luminous moon,
gibbous, glowing,
a pearl in velvet,
cream flesh against blue.
All acts of love are thine
(better if the moon is full).
Lady Valentine Moon,
today we celebrate love.

Tomorrow we march for peace.
How can men threaten war
on this day?
Missile kisses searing flesh;
caress of blood, shudder of bone,
spasm of sinew and corpuscle -
tumescent twisted bodies -
a little death.

After the act, desolation.
Women and men grieve, forsaken.
There is no resurrection -
ashes to ashes, dust to dust.
Only a promise
that one day we may meet,
and know, and remember,
and love again.

Valentine Moon,
valorous, unvanquished,

peaceful and peaceable,
silent and sacred;
demanding no sacrifice -
cast your light on warmongers.
Show them a shining world
glorious with love.

14/2/03

A day before the anti-Iraq war protest march

Aztec

Giant gods of stone
born from a rocky womb
spewed out of Popocatepetl
to cool at the world's bony rim.

The Plumed Serpent rises aflame,
monumental, from rivers of fire
a throbbing and bloody birth
cleaved with knife of obsidian and gold.

Here dances the Lord of Death –
in his ribs hangs the seat of the soul,
the liver, like some strange hard flower
budding in dusty ravine.

And she of the Serpent Skirt
grimaces gaunt-faced and fierce;
her scaly brood promising life
guarding Earth's vessels and bones.

Now our gentler, civilised gods
demand bloodier, deadlier deeds
pulping Earth's marrow, bleeding her dry
flaying her, skin by skin.

Can Coetlicue guard her still
or has she forever gone –
leaving her son, the god
of war, to terrify?

Where Are You Going?

Where are you going?
As far, as far, as far as I dare...
Down the stair and through the door-
I'll clasp moonbeams in my claws
and coat myself in silver, enough
to bristle feathers and sprout wings,
spark eyes, make a beak sharp as thorn.
I'll perch in the tallest tree, swivel my neck into night
and glide, soft as a sheet of snow
over the forest of dreams.

Where am I going?

As far, as far as a distant star -
Rigel, Altair, Alpheratz –
I'll soar past mansions of the moon.
Riding the plume of solar winds
I'll flame through constellations - Orion's Belt,
the Phoenix, Eagle, Crane and Bird of Paradise -
and free the Chained Princess, Andromeda,
before I spill my blood-red dust
in a dark nebula.

Mother, where are you going?

As far, as far, as far as I dare...

Blue Fish

Blue fish
you shimmer in my dreams;
behind my eyes, you coil
inside my brain.
You slip and slide, gliding
around corners of my consciousness –
as I turn to speak
or glance into the shadows
I catch suddenly
a snatch of blue, a flash
of fin, a twist
of tail, a glistening eye.

Sometimes
you are the vast ocean:
huge, endless, ceaseless
in your tides
pulling the undertow
of your fierce currents,
powerful in the curve
of sinew and muscle,
whirlpool and eddy.

Sometimes
you are the silence
of deep fathoms,
a press of darkness
and the weight of time:
you can feel
only your heart, barely beating
in the stillness.

Sometimes
you are playful,
thrashing bright water,
making spray churn
and glitter in the sun,
feeling each drop
of crystal ripple
down your skin.
We are born of water
you and I;
I am half-fish,
mermaid.

Tattoo Parlour

Sweeney Todd. The name
is no inducement
for body embellishment.
You must be brave
to enter this establishment –
cautiously as Bluebeard's wife,
resolute as an eco-warrior,
or brashly with a pirate's swagger.
Walk the plank with bravado –
submit to cutlass, pistol, needle,
cut-throat inks, red, plasma yellow,
blue, green, black
as a demon's evil
heart. You will depart
finely decorated,
alive or….
a hero.

Spring Orchids

The sun was pale and still,
grass damp with spring rain.
I walked uphill, towards the wood
above the cold grey town.
Suddenly I came upon
purple spotted lizard heads -
first one or two
then a dozen popped up
peering at me
above the grass.
Foreigners – so gaudy!
They eyed me warily
with hooded, golden,
alien eyes.
They told me they were
from another place;
explorers from beyond the stars
now left behind
to find a home.
I greeted them
in my best alien lizard tongue
and told them they were
welcome to stay.

Spring Equinox, Haweswater

High up, deer crop splintered grass
sculpted against stones and sky
and the brown bones of winter bracken.
A crucible of light burns on the lake.
Pools of stars dance and tremble
an ecstatic welcome for the young sun
while, far out, shadows of silver,
cobalt, indigo, are striped by wind.
The sky is duck-egg blue, with clouds
as softly tattered as fresh-hatched chicks
and in the feathered larches
chaffinches announce the spring.

Who knows
what this year will bring?
I dream of
new beginnings, new songs,
rich, unknown colours surging
across the lake, burnishing
the hills with amber,
gold, tourmaline, chrysoprase;
unimagined and mysterious shades
of a different world
blazing with possibilities.

Mother

At the start, it felt so easy,
natural, like sunlight in the trees
or apple blossom buds which swell
and burst their pools of foam,
radiant nectar for the waiting bees.

Sparrows have hidden secret nests
in the back lane. They guard their young
with a fierce pride, and bring them
to the feeders, all thin young awkward legs
and stubby beaks. At night the hedgehog
and her son poke and snuffle
contented in the woodpile.

When did it become so hard, to be a mother?
There is light and dark. The dark hangs heavy
and the pain is like a stone,
a slow pressure,
suffocation in the ribs,
a deep ache of bone.

Beltane

He sets the head alight,
Bel the bright one, child of the sun.

Now trees sing, and waterfalls of light
stream through the leaves
translucent in their newness.
Along hedgerows blackthorn cradles
blooms of foam, a portent
may blossom will soon follow.

After dark days we can still remember
to feel joy, chase dreams,
leap the Beltane fire, love
and dance in the woods.

The Year of the Tiger

This, the Year of the Water Tiger, is for courage.
It hurts that I don't know how your day goes,
who your neighbours are.
Are they kind to you?
What colour are your dreams,
do you find peace,
how is the food?

Six years ago, Year of the Fire Monkey and adventure,
we lazed by a beach, drinking cocktails
and watched the mango sun sink
into the sea. There was limbo dancing,
someone twirled fire sticks, we ate jack fruit and lychees,
pineapple, peaches, persimmons.

I found a photo of you on your balcony.
Behind you were mountains, and in the valley
cicadas were singing.
You were smiling.
It was your birthday.

The river here is wild
after spring storms. Cormorants, those small black dragons,
have lost their perch where water rages
over the pebbles.

Can you ever forgive me
for my fear of losing you?
Can you ever understand my terror?

There are rivers and mountains between us
and the earth is shaking.

This year, the Year of the Tiger, is for courage.

13/6/22

Midsummer

Midsummer pounced
like a stalking cat
with a swish of tail, and claws
as scythes slicing through time
and squeezing its life-blood
drop by drop.
A fierce propitiation.

Through a long cold spring
we had tried to imagine
hot hay-fields, lazy bees
and screams of swifts
piercing the blue dome of sky.
But we could not –
too slow the wheel's rotation.

Now suddenly she came -
Sunna, Sulis, bursting from her bed
a radiant bride, glowing and fulfilled
after a night of love.
Floating across the heavens
she flamed in her brief finery;
her secret, innermost parts
burning with seeds of winter and the dark.

Lady of the Links

Sea-borne, wind-blown,
storm-striven. On this north shore
you came from other worlds.
Shape-shifter.
From sand and stone
earth, shell, bone
you shaped your life
to your wild gods.
You danced the sands, spoke
with hogboons, sang with selkies,
tysties, loons. Moons waxed
and waned. From mists
you wove spells, rooting you
to this place of sky and stone.
The earth bloomed.
With corn and creel, bow and blade
you toiled, and with your kin
hefted, hewed to shape
the watchful goddess of your hearth.
You loved. A new birth. Seasons spun.
Storms raged and died.
Midwinter sun pierced
your inner chamber,
lovingly wrought;
stones shared your secrets.
A procession of skulls.
Death came early; but you
lay gentle on the earth,
flower-strewn. Skylarks sang.
Your spirit flew. Your breath
became the wind, your bones, jewels:
gold bedstraw, and a myriad pearls

      of eyebright.
   And on stormy days
   we hear your song;
     we see you
      dancing

Westray, Orkney - In honour of a figurine found in excavations of a Neolithic settlement on Westray.

Selkies = seals
Hogboons = earth spirits
Tysties = black guillemots
Loons = northern divers
Links = sand hills along the seashore
Link (v) = to dance or skip along

I Could Fly

Grass shimmered, a cracked mirror of green glass,
each blade a shard, sun shattered.
High overhead clouds hung, motionless fists
of candyfloss, abandoned
in a relentless sky. Trees smoked.
It was a day when
the earth flipped. As I blinked
my path tipped, and I slipped
through space into a forgotten, shining world.
Hills danced. Trees sang.
And I could fly.

Ta Prohm

Here the past ravels and unravels
under a canopy of light and dark, a forest
filled with murmurs of cicadas, whispers of a lost tribe.
We are stunned with heat. An ocean churns.
Demons glare. Towers crumble.

Our guide says *Many have vanished.*

Through the gateway
goddesses clasp lotus buds, refuse our gaze
to contemplate nirvana. We feel the press of vines,
the grip of strangler figs, a weight of pain.
Roots split stones. The sky falls.

My father was taken. It was Year Zero.

In the temple courtyard time stops.
Impossible trees stretch from ruins, trunks smooth
as silver, as tall as stars. Fat roots
snake over tiled roofs, pour down pillars, squeeze walls.
Breath rattles. Life-blood soaks away.

Many vanished, but we have survived.

A monk gives blessings
and the musk of incense follows us, bittersweet. The trees
embrace bones, cradle the world, the sky, the ravages of loss.
Moon-white spider lilies glow fragrant along the path.
Lizards bask. Bee-eaters sing.

Ta Prohm is one of the Angkor temples in Cambodia, the "jungle temple" used in the film "Tomb Raider".

Year Zero was the year (1975) Cambodia was taken over by the Khmer Rouge.

Climbing, Floating, Flying

We climbed the Peak at night, and saw stars flaming at our feet, burning

in a bowl as if the sky was upside down. In the shop

you broke a statue of a warrior – shattered, he could not defend

the Emperor, but lay crushed like petals trampled on a battlefield.

Dismayed, we beat a slow retreat, to creaks and rattles in the tram,

like Mah Jong pieces tipsy on a sliding board, among bright towers

which squeezed old temples, hidden plots of banyans and bamboos.

Antique oracles. Ancient wounds.

On the Star Ferry to Kowloon

our spray-pierced hearts pooled and rocked in opium dark waters.

In Stanley and Repulse the Tao blessed us with flowers of fortune -

chrysanthemum and lotus, water lanterns, gauzy atolls

floating on the bay, unruffled and mysterious as wispy-bearded sages

cradling our souls to safety. Children stroked dragons. Crowds poured between white pillars carved in light. We crossed the Bridge of Longevity, and flew

exultant with Tin Hau, Queen of Heaven, into the vastness of the day.

Stone Forest I

Bougainvillea

blazed, paper lanterns trembling,

smoking in hot air.

Stone Forest II

Rock canopies grew,

gigantic, silent, guarding

a wise, ancient land.

The Hill of the Witch

Lammas,
we climbed the Hill of the Witch
eastwards
with the young sun.
But we were unwelcome;
she was displeased, or startled
by our hasty homage -
conjuring Morrigan mist,
wild raven winds,
hissing serpent rain
to hide her grim throne.
We turned west
and with the sun,
(he now fiery and mature)
were granted audience.
The stones sparkled, larks sang,
and inside the chamber portals
spiders spun cocoons over
seven secret recesses.
The tall crystal pillar
glistened palely,
penetrating the darkness.

August 2002   *Visit to the Hill of the Witch, Loughcrew, Co Meath,*

Do You Remember?
(For Leena)

Do you remember the rackety bus
and the old pock-marked road?
The secret path to the house
around the ribbed pine roots, sunshine
on the veranda, the old well?
The smell of hot pines, and birch leaves in the sauna?
How they loved to garden, fighting roots and rocks,
growing fat marrows like a miracle
and beetroots tasting of earth?
We had our own gardens.
I think mine did better than yours!
I had forget-me-nots, and once
I grew a runner-bean inside a tin.
We fed hedgehogs, and the grass-snake we named Emma
who came shyly down to the shore
with her young. We hid behind a rock,
watching their gentle, flicking tongues, the delicate way
they slid around the stones.
We picked plump bilberries in the forest
staining our hands and lips purple
like vampires, and imagined wolves
and witches and gingerbread houses.
On the rocks we built houses of reindeer moss.
Years later you told me I liked the scarlet cranberry leaves
with gold crinkled edges – I had forgotten.
We had rock pools, and I collected crystal stones
that glittered under the water,
Did you collect those? I can't remember.
I remember how, when I took the stones out of the water,
they stopped glittering.
I teased you, I remember that.

Sometimes we were both in trouble
and sent outside to repent. Once we got lost
in the forest, only a short distance from the house -
I can still feel that grip of fear.
Do you remember the anaconda pond?
So deep, it went down
to fathomless, murky depths
full of the lurking terrors of childhood.
But mostly I remember sunshine and laughter,
your mother making *pulla* in the kitchen,
the wind in the pines
and eating sugar wrapped in lettuce leaves.
Do you?

Pulla: Sweet Finnish bread flavoured with cardamum

The House at Päiväranta

Memories of a Finnish Childhood

Years ago, my friend Leena told me she was going to try to write something about our childhood. More particularly, about our summer holidays together on an island in Finland, and some of the events from that time, so long ago. She even mentioned Mad Cow Island. Imagine - things that happened nearly 70 years ago! Almost three-quarters of a century. I sometimes feel as if they occurred to someone else, wrapped as they are in a veil of distance and time. Then a glitter of sunlight on water, the resinous smell of pine trees, the taste of a wild bilberry, and I am transported back as if by a wave of a magic wand.

As a young child I lived with my father, in a city called Turku, in south-west Finland. Leena lived with her mother and aunt on the other side of town. We didn't see a lot of each other for much of the year, but in the summer we shared a cottage on an island in the Turku archipelago. The archipelago consists of chains of islands sprinkled like jewels into the Baltic Sea, reaching half-way to Sweden. The largest islands are wooded, with pockets of fertile soil, and in those days dotted with small farms. Each house or farm had its sauna, built by the shore, and on Saturday evenings you would see the smoke rising from the sauna chimneys, as each family lit the woodburning stoves in readiness for their ritual ablutions. Surrounded by sea, everyone used boats to get about, and learnt to row from a young age. I can still hear the familiar sound, the "put-put-put" of the old motor boats chugging sedately along. Life in general seemed to proceed at a much slower and more tranquil pace. We had more time for each other, says Leena. There were fewer distractions.

I have known Leena almost all my life. I think of her as my oldest friend, someone who shared my happiest childhood memories, someone I can share my thoughts and feelings with even in our increasingly mature years. This is in spite of the fact that we are over 1000 miles apart, and only see each other on average every 6 years (longer now). Of course now we have modern technology to help us – emails, phone texts, skype, and (horrors) even facebook! These things were inconceivable in our childhood, where many people didn't even have a telephone. But as children we shared something special, which I find very difficult to describe –

something like "the spirit of the Finnish countryside," and this has shaped us into the people we have become.

The smooth, rounded rocks you can see along the shore-line of Päiväranta are made of pink granite, with dark flecks and flashes of sparkling crystal. Leena once told me she imagined giants living there. But I wonder if pieces of the *sampo,* the magic mill that wily old wizard Väinämöinen tried to steal from the Witch of the North, aren't hidden under the stones. If you lie on the sauna rock you can feel the energy pulsing and humming underneath you. One day Louhi, the Witch Queen of the North, may come to reclaim her magic.

Leena doesn't look like a typical Nordic blonde. She is dark, with large brown eyes and a snub nose. Of course now there is grey in the hair. I am the blonde these days! We are neither of us tall and slim – we are both a lot more rounded than we used to be! She often has a mischievous look in her eyes, and has a wicked sense of humour. When we were young I used to tease her a lot and boss her around, as I was the oldest, but she has got her own back on me many times since then...

I remember a particular long, hot summer. But then, all summers seemed to be long and hot, merging into each other, stretching enticingly and timelessly ahead, full of the promise of adventure and the unknown. As we had no car, my father and I travelled out to the island by bus – or rather, two buses and two ferries. We finished the journey by motor boat, brought out to meet us by a neighbour, the farmer who lived near the cottage. In those days the roads were rough and rutted, and the buses rattled and shook, bucking and heaving like untamed horses. I always felt travel-sick, but somehow it didn't matter, because I was so excited to be going to Päiväranta. This means "Day-shore", and to me as a 6 or 7 year-old it meant the same as Paradise.

Approaching by sea from Rymättylä, where the bus had dropped us, we could see the rounded granite outcrop of our sauna rock with the sauna building perched beside it, and further in the red tiled roof of the cottage nestling among the pine trees. On the jetty our friends Pirkko and Kaija were waiting for us, and Leena was running up and down and waving excitedly. They had travelled over some days previously, in order to meet with the carpenter, who was busy working on the house. He had just finished the wooden bunk beds in the attic, and was now working on the steps and seating of the verandah.

"Come and see our new beds!" shouted Leena, and took me up the steep outside wooden staircase to the attic, smelling of fresh pine and birchwood. The bunk beds fitted cosily under the sloping roof. Up there were toys, a doll's house, and lots of books. Years later, we found one called "Invisibility: Mastering the Art of Vanishing," and spent a hilarious evening joking about how we would use it to visit each other without having to pay the fare. I still have the book, but have to admit I've never managed to master that art.

When the verandah was finished we had most of our meals there. Leena's mother, Kaija, was a wonderful cook, and one of my lasting memories was of her making bread, fragrant buns and bilberry pies early in the morning, and the whole cottage being filled with the delicious aroma of baking. We ate lots of fish, as these were abundant, and fishing was an important activity in our life among the islands; we caught perch and bream, and my father once caught an enormous pike. I remember that after it was killed, Kaija gutted it there on the rocks, and the heart was still beating – it glistened wetly on the rock, pumping up and down like a small, demented bellows. I was horrified, but also fascinated. I worried about the feelings of the pike – was it really dead? But this was part of the fabric of life then. The pike got cooked and eaten, anyway.

Leena and I spent many happy hours splashing about in the sea. I used to collect sparkling granite stones and use them to make rock pools and underwater gardens. Someone gave us some large inner tyres which we used as floats, and this provided endless fun. At other times, we built houses made with reindeer moss, which grew on all the rocks. Late in the summer there were expeditions to pick mushrooms and bilberries, which grew abundantly in the forest surrounding the house. And we had expeditions in the rowing boat, rowing out to some of the neighbouring islands, many of which were uninhabited. That was how we came to visit Mad Cow Island. But that's another story. Maybe Leena will write it.

And she has!

The Sauna at Päiväranta

Mad Cow Island

It was on one of those beautiful sunny summer days of our childhood that we all were going to have a picnic. Me, my little friend Lissa, her father Geoffrey, my mother Kaija and my auntie Pirkko. By the rowing boat to an island to pick bilberries.

My mother was on kitchen duty and we had boiled eggs and things as usual for breakfast. Everybody wanted their eggs cooked differently, so every egg in the pan had a picture on its side. Little stick figures describing the owner one way or the other. Candy, the six-toed cat, was prowling under the table waiting for a bare ankle to strike his sharp teeth and nails into. (He loved to do that to our guests, especially the female ones to cause a screaming and kicking fit that made the things on the table fly. Maybe he still remembered the very traumatic day he was brought to Päiväranta in a sack, for whiskers' sake!)

When everything was packed, from picnic basket to pillows to sit on in the boat, we got on the way, Pirkko taking one oar and Kaija the other. Geoffrey was in the back and Lissa and I in the front.

We got to an island, later to be called The Mad Cow Island for a reason. My mother and auntie got their berry picking gear – baskets for Kaija and Pirkko, and also a light green pan for Pirkko in case there were lots of berries, which she wore on her head, like a metal hat. And there were a lot of berries, which got bigger the further they went in to the middle of the island, never mind a barbed-wire fence and a couple of cows. An old one with massive horns and a younger cow. Mother and daughter maybe.

But who is worried about cows, not those two. And maybe the old cow was friendly, but got suspicious and worried about the green pan on my auntie's head. It started to huff and puff and paw the ground. And it started to charge at Pirkko, who jumped over the fence but the cow, now definitely very angry, followed. Pirkko made a rapid turn to the right when she reached the young alders and willows by the beach and ran as fast as she could towards Lissa and me, threw us in the boat from the sand where we were happily playing by the boat. We didn't know what was going on and why we were thrown into the boat in such a hurtful way and naturally started to howl. Geoffrey, who was fishing nearby on a rock, looked up in astonishment and asked in a nonchalant way if there was a snake in somebody's boot.

In the meantime Kaija had crawled under the barbed-wire fence and tried to approach the beach. The cow, who had been tangled in the bushes got loose, noticed her and rushed after her. Kaija had no other choice than go into the water and start swimming with the bilberry basket between her teeth. The cow followed her for quite a while, but finally gave up and the poor wet woman was able to clamber into the boat.

This story has turned into a legend of The Mad Cow Island in my family and was told by Pirkko numerous times during the coming years. This is how I remember it.

Leena Karjalainen

Next page: Memories of Childhood

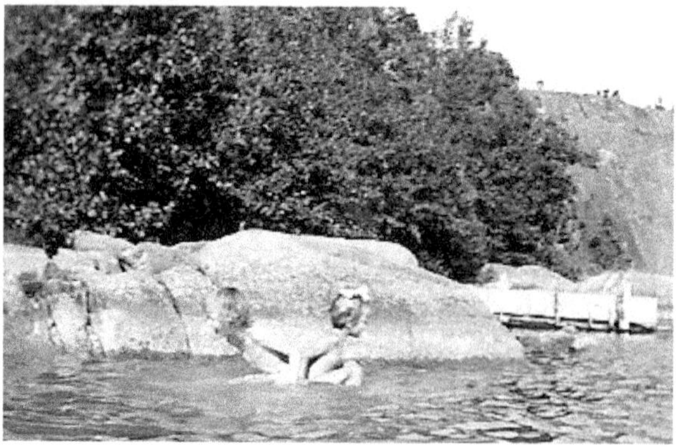

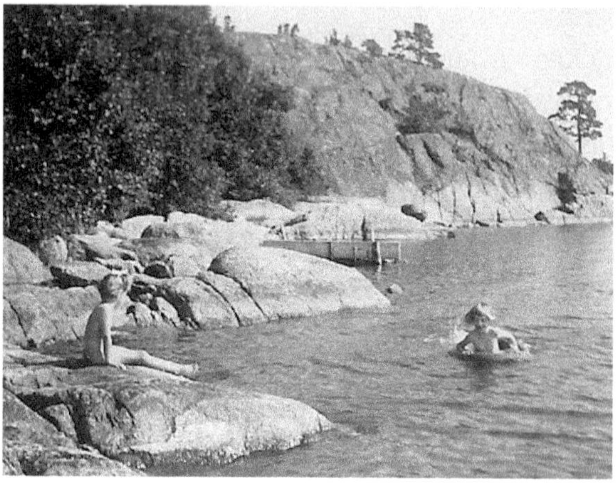

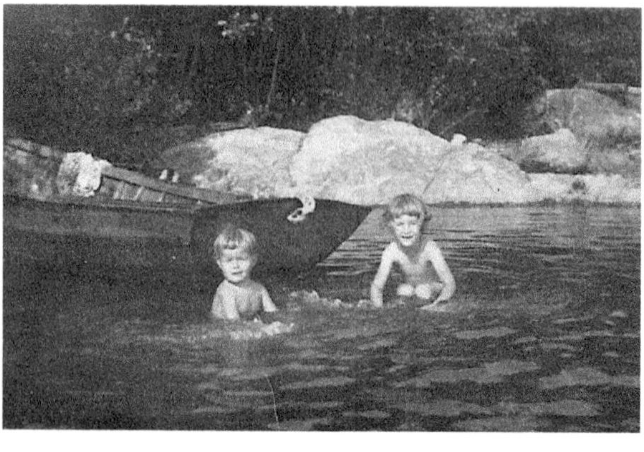

Sycorax

Hast thou forgot
the foul witch Sycorax ...
Shakespeare: The Tempest

Her skin sprouts black feathers,
her lips ossify. She has become
hideous in her sorrow, scratching
the dust-dry tracks with pitchy claws,
pecking scraps of bones,
eating the dead.

Her memories leak like tears - a city
white as milk beside a turquoise sea,
where minarets spin light, and cedars
shade gardens heavy with musk
of jasmine, neroli, attar of rose.

Her mind scatters, pools.

I once ruled the moon, the ebb and flow
of ocean, tides of blood;
I held a sea god in my arms –
I was more powerful than a summer storm.

The island was mine.
Mine and my son's.

Now she remembers
his breath brushing her cheek,
his fists tight as buds, the smell
of his hair like moss on fire;
his dancing legs, his wildness
and his secret ways.

She perches on the tallest pine, watching
the snakeskin sea, the close
but empty sky. She has forgotten why
she waits, why she feels such loss,
why all she's known
is vanishing.

Autumn Equinox

Fat pods pop
expelling tight black seeds
like bursts of antimatter
firing to the dark stars.
In autumn the earth spins
away from light towards the source
where darkness and brightness
fold inwards in eternity.
Star children, we have blown
in endless space
and grown from incandescent stellar dust
to bloom, luxuriant and fierce,
riding careless the solar winds
in this small universe.
Now, as the axis moves about the Pole
and the Great Bear slowly turns,
we split our veil of flesh,
exploding through the Tears of Pleiades
and sow our brief atoms
along the Milky Way.

Roar Like a Lion

Your rage is an ache
        a darkness within me.
I don't know how
        to live with it.
What can I say?
        I'm sorry.
I will always care.
        Love is pain.

Now you can roar
like a lion, stand proud
on that rock and roar –
make the earth tremble.

Your anger
        gives you wings.
A fire dragon
        you can fly
into the future.

One day I hope
there will be forgiveness.
But if not,
as long as you can roar and fly
perhaps that's all
that matters.
But it hurts.
It hurts.

Companions *(For Keith)*

We have travelled a long way together –
north, south, west and east.
We have been good companions,
walking the wilds, exploring
by foot, on trains and boats and planes…

We've tramped the hills and moors
of Cumbria and Yorkshire, watched sunsets
in Orkney and Cornwall. We've seen
fluorescent seas, feral goats, a vitreous fort,
burial chambers and stone circles…

In the north we reached Finland,
Portugal in the west, Italy the south,
Borneo and China in the east.
And so many places in between.
We have trekked and journeyed far.

Now we are content to walk leisurely
in the lane, admire flowers
in the garden, watch birds at the feeders;
especially our gang
of garrulous sparrows.

We look out for the hedgehogs
snuffling along the path.
We talk to friends and neighbours.
We continue to be
good companions.

The Journey

I am a traveller on a road
which winds the earth
and journeys to the stars.
At first the path was smooth
as beech-buds in a winter wood:
all was possibility, latent, new.
Along the way a hawthorn hedge or two
were thorny, but the blossom
smelt of heaven, and wayside flowers
gravely nodded greetings.
The path grew steeper,
twisting here and there
past boulders beating their hard drums
of duty, dedication and desire,
and streams, singing of love and hate and fear,
rippled the mountainside with dreams.
There were summer isles
crowned with fragrant pines,
and deserts of hot sand and stones
scorching each step
and parching lips and bones.
There was the bluest ocean once;
and by the shore a house
where bougainvillea blazed and smoked
like paper lanterns on a summer's night.

I have walked through forest
where sunlight scatters
into sprays of light
and all is hushed, except a crack
of twig, or howl of wolf;

here are dim shapes
of things that were, or might have been,
or things to come – a witch's spell,
a house of gingerbread,
a mighty stag, proud, tall,
watchful in the shadows.

Where will the journey end?
Perhaps by boat across the sea
or in the mountains, near the sky;
or in this meadow, laced with buttercups
and drones of bees, and cries of swifts.
I will fly then, to the stars.

Immram

Dying leaves, husks of the year's passions
flame and gutter, blown like brittle sparks
from a cold forge - gold, copper, sulphur, iron,
crimson as blood to brown as bitter bile.
High above broods Black Combe, Anu of the mists,
goddess of twilight and the dark;
panther guardian of the western gate –
must I pass her fierce gaze before travelling on?

My immram, my soul journey, now begins
beyond the ninth wild wave, to speed
towards that dread source, a dance as hard
as stone, as bare as bone, the end of all desire.
A hooded heron guides me, down to the shingle shore –
silver-grey as the sea which shifts and rasps
the glass-smooth pebbles of the churning mill,
ceaseless and desolate as seagulls' cries.

My crew are singing swans and gulls,
arrow-sharp gannets keen as Nuada's sword,
and terns with crescent wings scything the vast voids
of space between the sea and distant stars.
Bridled by serpents scaly bright
my craft is sturdy, dragon-beaked;
I need to trust her power to steer
past rocky islands of the Otherworld.

Sometimes I must step ashore, fearful
of cannibal horses, giant ants, the Revolving Beast
which turns its bones within the skin
shuddering like a shaman's bag.
I dare cross the net of mist, gateway

to four worlds of form and flow, dragons, fiery pigs,
Guardians of the Circled Fire –
a flaming forge of alchemy and light.

I feel the fire inside my ribs;
alien pulse of power and fear
freezing blood, vein, lymph: heart of hearts,
bone, sinew, marrow, chilled as ice.
I am afraid of the year's death, the pyre
of skeleton leaves smouldering in cold soil,
the spent carcase settling in ocean's ooze –
wreck of spring's promise, hopes unfulfilled.

Now I must hurry in my quest between
the worlds, between sea and wind and rocks and fearful fire
to do those things that must be done
before winter, and the hard journey's end.
As dawn breaks, the crucible of sky makes sun's
gold tears glisten; spring will come again –
and from the pyre's ashes rise dragons.
Overhead a falcon hovers; here is landfall.

Hecate

It's time to make my peace with Hecate –
she who guards the gates of death, seeks
lost travellers in the underworld,
mother of witches and angels;
goddess of boundaries.

She found my daughter, who blazed
a path in autumn, walked
over roof-tops and flew through clouds –
lioness of courage, touched by the moon,
precious as life.

Hecate, show me your third face
so I can ride again the wild spaces;
I have run with your hounds, and felt
the smooth slithered skin of a serpent
coiled at my heart.

I want to gallop across ravines, savour
jolts of straining muscle, heave of lung,
remembering my old fierce life
before you come for me, whispering
your last spells.

When you unlock your sanctuary's door
I will follow. But before that, let me
dance the spiral, beat a drum,
circle the fire, watch stars – allow me
to love this world.

We Are The Witches

We are the flow, we are the ebb...
We are the witches back from the dead.
                    Shekhinah Mountainwater

It was hard, the incarnation.
First, the gathering of gallows' dust, ashes and scatterings
of life shed under an ebbing moon
in cellars, city streets and hill-tops, churches,
forest hovels, palaces and prisons -
here is the rack, strappado, fire, the iron shoes.
A search for bones worn smooth on river beds
or bog-stained, buried among flowers and mud.

Then, the slow build of bone on bone,
of flesh on flesh, an interlace of sinew and taut threads
of muscle spun with charms from spiders' webs.
We heard the call and trembled -
Isis, Astarte, Diana, Hecate
the salty taste of iron in our veins, the pumping
of our hearts, the singing of our blood.
Hecate, Demeter, Kali, Inanna.

How far we had to travel! We journeyed in the dark,
in twilight, nightshade, moonshine, to a place
that was not a place, between the worlds...
We rode eggshells over water, flew with sticks and stones
until at last we dared to fly
like eagles towards the sun.